First published in the UK in 2012

First Edition April 2012

Publisher Sharon Diana Abel

ISBN 978-0-9567248-2-3
Nielson

A TABLESPOON OF BITTERSWEET

Table of Contents

A tablespoon of bittersweet

Another drop of sadness
A sifting of regret
Half an ounce of memories
Blended to forget

A tablespoon of bittersweet
Extra measure of mistrust
Pound or two of despair
The mixture made robust

Drain off expectation
Knead with downward thumb
Whisked in to obscurity
Baked to firm and numb

Addiction

Another puff
To punish, destroy
My worthiness
To curb the hunger, the yearning

Another thought
Dissecting the cryptic message
Interpreted in negativity
'Will have to take a rain cheque'
It reads

Something to be said
To the love of your life?
Not likely
Not worthy

Another puff
Leading to addiction
Of self loathing
Self contempt

Reading again
A brush off perhaps?
No 'Babe', no 'darling'
No recognition
No answers

Spiralling smoke
Gone in a moment
The briefest pleasure
Wafting away

Dispersing hope
Wilting dreams
The fantasy evaporates
Floating into past

'Will have to put tonight on hold'
Speaking volumes
Left suspended in time
Left in limbo

The future split
In my mind

Which direction
Will the clouds unfurl
Which poison, intoxication
Will be my demise

Again

I look to the future
And see the past

I see the now
As it once was

I know what's altered
Hasn't changed

I won't go down that road
Again

I hold the man
That I once held

It all feels new
Though it is old

Re-written by the same device
Recycled maybe once or twice

I won't go down that road
Again

All the Daughters

Born of strength
From union of pleasure
Controversy

Shielded by great warrior
Defended by ally
In battle
Cradle to grave

Confronting injustice
With nurture by side
Sharing in triumph
Regaling tales
To reminisce

Heeding wise words
Which heal
Sealing bond
That binds

Bailed from hardship
Unconditional
Guardian of her spoils
Her riches

Nursed, from penetrating
Open wounds
Of all weary
All life

Shadowy counterpart
Mirrored through eyes
Reflecting image
Of the heroine

Between the lines

I saw the look
Coy smiles, eyes dropped
The secrecy

Talk of news
With lingering words
Lingering meaning

Lips parting, through silent pause
Drawing each other closer
Breathing in the scent

Fidgeting, with hair, with hands
Desire to be touched
To touch

Inviting one another to cross
The invisible line
Weakening
Masks slipping

I saw it all
Played in mind
In your minds
Between the lines

Can You Accept

Can you embrace

With absolute abandon

My yesteryear

Under wraps

Of tarnished layers

Thrown into odium

Once revealed

My glory days

May stain you

Prepared to share?

Endorse the revelations?

The shame of yore

Now prided in memory

Origins which led me

From naivety, apathy

Can you feel honour

In my disclosure

Bring me from my seclusion

Welcome the past

The now?

Collision Course

Destined to collide
From complicated web
To meet
Absorb the lessons
From each and everyone

Our pathway, routed
On the footpath, enlightened
Off course along the way
Through the maze
Of interactions

Woven in wires
Of formed attachments
Fleeting knowing
Channelling to you

Entanglement along the way
Veering off track
Building impressions
Which drive me

Grasping the chain
Of latticed diversion
To gain clear sight
The ultimate goal
And clash along the way
To enrich

Defeated

Dying
Slowly dying
On the spot
In the moment

Another knock back
Wounded
Wrenching gut
Reinforcing images
Of no use
Non-descript
Dispensable

There to be mauled
By words ferocious
Formed on barbed tongue

Melting
Slowly melting
To non- existence
Of no importance

Snatched delusions
Of overcoming.
Ideals of triumph
To be ripped apart
In cruel revelry

Drowning
Slowly drowning
In introspect
To wallow
In self absorption

Pushed aside
Out of favour
Un-extraordinary occurrence
To those unaffected

Crawling
Slowly crawling
Back to defeat
To perish

Granny's House

Small small child, eyes wide
Any tears, now dried
Arrived!

So big, so warm, so much at peace
This candy house is full of dreams

Red, white paving front
Stepping stones, to jump upon
Huge bay windows, peer inside
Curtains hanging, bold and bright

Out the back the long, long shed
Must be careful where to tread
So many treasures, buried deep
Adventures, playing hide 'n seek

Laughter, running upon the grass
Flowers form a pretty path
White trellis fence, to keep them safe
From little feet that stamp and race

Through patio doors a piano sits
Tempted fingers want to flit
Heavy lid opened, explored
Legs sway and dangle off the floor

Upstairs, the epitome of fun
The biggest bed to jump upon
Aroma of the crisp white sheets
Encouraging a peaceful sleep

Dressing table, White and gold
Where sat, and many stories told
Pretty mirrors, little drawers
Trinkets, bottles
Gaze in awe

Delicious smells, that waft upstairs
From the kitchen, food's prepared
Huge pots and pans, allowed a taste
A lesson, making marmalade

Hugs and chatter, time to go
Outside the door
The stepping stones

Extinguish the light

The need to sleep for days
For weeks
For ever

Float away in tepid stream
Yawn in sopor
To hibernate in finality

Dance with Morpheus
In land of dreams
Eternal rest

Extinguish from slumber
In permanent demise
Intoxicated
With departure
To bow a graceful exit
In peak of life

A being, moribund
Favouring the numbness
Awakened
In expiration

Faithless

Stamping your insecurities
Upon vulnerabilities
I'd tried to overcome

Don't make me surrender
To your cynicism
Be weakened by your dubiety

You've formed your opinion
Should I fight
To clear your presumptions?
Dissuade your mistrust?
Subservient to your influence?

A shadow you carry with you
Forcing others
To plead their innocence

Won't bow to your annoyance
Misguided hunches
Your lack of faith speaks volumes
But not of me

Games Master

Let the games begin
To intimidate, ridicule
Abuse his power
Of position, craving

Sadistic in his intellect
Wants to play
With her misery
In hostile isolation

His outer pleasantries
Concealing caustic intention
Towards his victim
His pastime

Surely spending twilight hours
Plotting her demise, subservience
She will pay
In ways undetected
Devious, scheming
To rattle her mind

Him competitive, though she is not
competing
Cunning goes unchallenged
His contest alone
As she obeys his surly command
Scathing words
Disguised in harmful sham

Underhanded strategy
To wear away her optimism
He is amused
At her discomfort
His scoring of words

As in childhood
She faces the menacing brutish bully
Used to entertain
Chased into submission
Feels the acid rain
Prickling the damaged nerves
Eroding all confidence

All for his diversion

Over enthused with others
Welcoming, agreeable
The hidden sly fox
Revelling in mischief
Snide prankster
With ploy to belittle
He is winning

She is Cast out
Into the cold, crisp reality

This alien intent cannot be halted
Desire cannot be quelled
Hooked on her suffering
His grand plan

Feeding off his tactics
With spiteful victory
Smug in the knowledge
Of what he has created

Part of her now
Beneath her skin, crawling
She'll learn her lesson
What was the lesson?

Beyond reason, beyond purpose
Toying with the damage
His outlet, his release
The games go on
Undiscovered

Grittier side

Did you expect Roses
To bloom at your wake
Fanfare of trumpeters
To celebrate?!

All sweetness and light?
Those around you enriched?
Adoration, true meaning?
'aint life a bitch!

Did you think it so easy
So free, so serene
Thought they'd understand you?
Nope, they're heartless, they're green

Ha! You believed in unconditional
Stand by grittier side
When rock bottom hits
All you have is inside

Did you misunderstand
Bitterly rebuff
The hand of an optimist
To savage the trust

Thought it was a breeze
Those rich spoils of life
Did you think it was costless?
Did you not see the price?

What did you expect?
An easy smooth ride?
To sail off in delirium
With life's bonny tide...

How Did You Know?

You held out your hand
I took it
Snatched it up
Who sent you?
How did they know?

You threw a lifeline
I hadn't asked for
Though needed
Though desperate
Why did you do that?

You gave without taking
I cherished it
Just in time
You saved me
How did you know?

If I Could

If I could sing it
It would harmonise
The skies of song
In lyrical clouds
Tones of yearning
Echo through the atmosphere
Of reciprocation

If I could paint it
A masterpiece
Of visual tales
Depicting vibrant mix of colour
Dark, desperate ache
Etched deeply
Into canvass

If I could write it
My outpour
Would hypnotise
Tug the chords of longing
Exposed in language
Expressions un-cloaked

If I could show it
In tender form
Eyes revealing, unconditional
Drawing in
To clasp, embrace
Applaud in celebration

If I could just
Say it

Magnetised

I am intoxicated
With your utterings
Stemming from deep thoughts
Deep understanding

Worldly wise
Intelligence exudes
Towards me

Penetrating knowledge
Mastered talents
Which inspire
Draw me to you

To travel in your mind
Read the unreadable
Synapses of wonderment
Charged, to allure
Tug my yearnings
Towards you

Magnetised in every particle
I gravitate in vice like grip
Connected

Sharp in comprehension
In wit, in brilliance
To reason philosophies
Strung in language
Of mine

Suspicion

Creeping into my veins
Snarling, unfurling
Clawing, gnawing under skin
Eating away all trust
Breaking out
Into hives of realization
Hell-bent on the satisfaction of proof

Suspicion

Obvious trail of deception
Had I been misled
By optimistic foolery!
Stupidity

But wait
Perhaps a little hasty
Perhaps a little wantant
To tip the tower of hope
Masochistic in my glory
In quest for truth

Delving into the negative
Make me right

Make me wrong

Suspicion

Manic

Unleashed, unbolted
Deflation of inner conflict
Muting of pain, confusion
Of frustration, self-reliance
Pressure, foreboding
Desperate doom

Starved of saviour
Starved of food
Delirium, hypoxia
Need to escape
Into a surreal world

Creativity flowing like medicine
Risk upon risk to appease
Ramblings of grand schemes
They listen, attentive
To calm, join the charade

But they don't know
Do they?
Am I aware
Of what is noticed

My control slipping
Or steadfast, rigid
Throwing away what's good

Sleep secondary
Can't quell the creativity
Whilst at its peak
Before the crash
The inevitable

The Confidante

That 'quiet word in your ear'
That focus
Look past it
Dissect it

That player, for her own ends
Which you misinterpret
The goals in mind
Are for her gain alone

Shrewd in manipulation
Craft in all her intuition

In guise of confidante to most
To absorb, take their inspiration
Passing as her own
To get closer
To her prize

Back exposed
To less worthy pursuits
And you, moulded
Blinded

Misdirected in your accusations
Feeds her smugness
Her twisted game

That power of suggestion
Planting thoughts into your mind
Be cautious
Who's words you speak
Who's gaze you hold

That 'quiet word in your ear'?
That focus?
Look past it
See through it

Underbelly of the Beast

Allow me to harness it
Your softer side
Oozing from beneath your shell
Stoked from underbelly
Of the beast

Let me coax the sweetness
Cultivate into my delight
Free that which you store
To remain captive in me

Can I relish in your extracts
Store your honey
So I may bask in its containment

Grant its liberty
On days like these
Your softer side
From underbelly
Of the beast

Tormentor

Deep in chatter
She holds her own
Laughing, she overcame
Triumphed the deep-seated
Tumbling thoughts

Winning the war
Of inner conflict
Outwardly

Turning to the door ajar
She sees the catalyst
Enter, smiling

The chatter slows
Moment frozen, shattered
Into a million piercing pieces

Recoiled in pain
Recognition

He is here

Casting doubt, disgust
She, still fragile it seems
From the calculated
Cold manipulation

Thoughts tumble once more
Scattered, scathing
Bravado shrinking

His eyes bore in

She remembers
He remembers

Does he soak up the fear

The threat

Intrusion into her sanity

Barging into the façade

Crashing around her

In silent turmoil

He is free, recharged

Exhibits warmth

Through cold cold gaze

His secret safe

Wealth of Life

I've dined with Princes, on foreign sands
Resided in squats within this land
Met, and mingled with fortune and fame
Shared pots of tea with pimps and Dames!

I've stood on steely wings of flight
Lived off the land, yet soared so high
Entertained the masses, impressed the few
Experienced the old, the new

I've seen emotions at their peak
Grown strong, made weak
Displayed my art, displayed my skill
Praised the great, soothed the ill

Met those who conquer, those who stagnate
Accomplished in what they consummate
The saintly good, the twisted bad
The explorer who was slightly mad

Teachers, poets, actors galore
Soldiers, courtesans and more
Dancers, singers, business folk
The wealth of life they still provoke

What Do You See?

Look at me
Look hard
Deep
Do you see a person?
With human needs?

Your savage thoughts
Steely, penetrating
Selfish

Just flesh, such flesh
To consume
In carnivore lust
To feed
On vulnerability

To knead and fondle
Bruise and mould

Slot into place
A fitting position

Useful to degree
For a moment

Look past the now
Past the cardinal

Calm the chaos
In your loins
Stem the imbalance
Steady your ardour

Now, look at me
Properly!

When I Am...

When I am slim
My strength will shine
Such health, such vigour
Lain dormant for an age
Released in abundant energy
To sparkle, to unleash
The agile being
Once locked, confined

When I am slender
So neat and trim
I'll dazzle, in the tightest dress
Draw gasps of adoration
From waiting crowds
Come, follow my example
Be seen with me
Breathtaking! Statuesque!
Untouchable

When I am slight
Success will come
Accomplished in my self-denial
Focused and at peak
See my drive
My supremacy
Refined in self-control
To be admired in my triumph

When I am frail
Such envy of my dainty frame
Bitter words, cloaked in kindness
And yet, at last
Feeling delicate, exquisite
As I should
To be nurtured, cherished
Ravenous for acceptance

When I am feeble
Wanting for nothing
No hankerings, no longings

No desire

“She is worn, she is withered”
So they’ll say
Empty, hollow
So they’ll say

Victorious
I will say....

Previous Publications
By Sharon D Abel

Secrets And Seductions

ISBN 978-0-9567248-0-9 Nielson October 2010

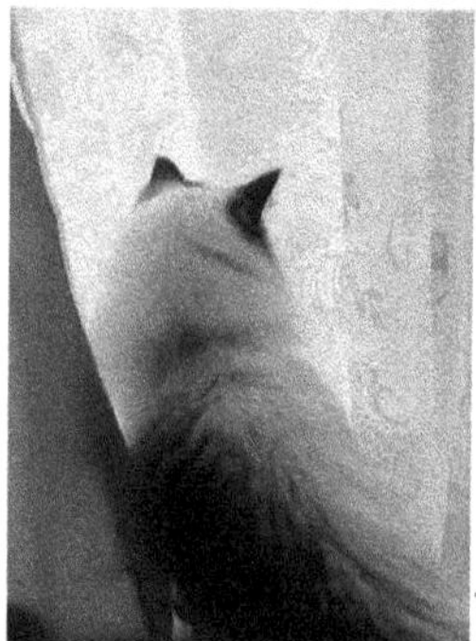

Dolly Finds Her Riches

ISBN 978-0-9567248-1-6 Nielsen April 2012

www.ingramcontent.com/pod-product-compliance
Ingram Content Group UK Ltd.
Pitfield, Milton Keynes, MK11 3LW, UK
UKHW020231250726
13967UKWH00001B/296